My Autism Book

of related interest

Inside Asperger's Looking Out
Kathy Hoopmann
ISBN 978 1 84905 334 1
eISBN 978 0 85700 670 7

All Cats Have Asperger Syndrome
Kathy Hoopmann
ISBN 978 1 84310 481 0

Can I tell you about Asperger Syndrome?
A guide for friends and family
Jude Welton
Illustrated by Jane Telford
Part of the Can I tell you about...? series
ISBN 978 1 84310 206 9
eISBN 978 1 84642 422 9

Different Like Me
My Book of Autism Heroes
Jennifer Elder
Illustrated by Marc Thomas and Jennifer Elder
ISBN 978 1 84310 815 3
eISBN 978 1 84642 466 3

The ASD Workbook
Understanding Your Autism Spectrum Disorder
Penny Kershaw
ISBN 978 1 84905 195 8
eISBN 978 0 85700 427 7

My Child Has Autism, Now What?
10 Steps to Get You Started
Susan Larson Kidd
ISBN 978 1 84905 841 4
eISBN 978 0 85700 349 2

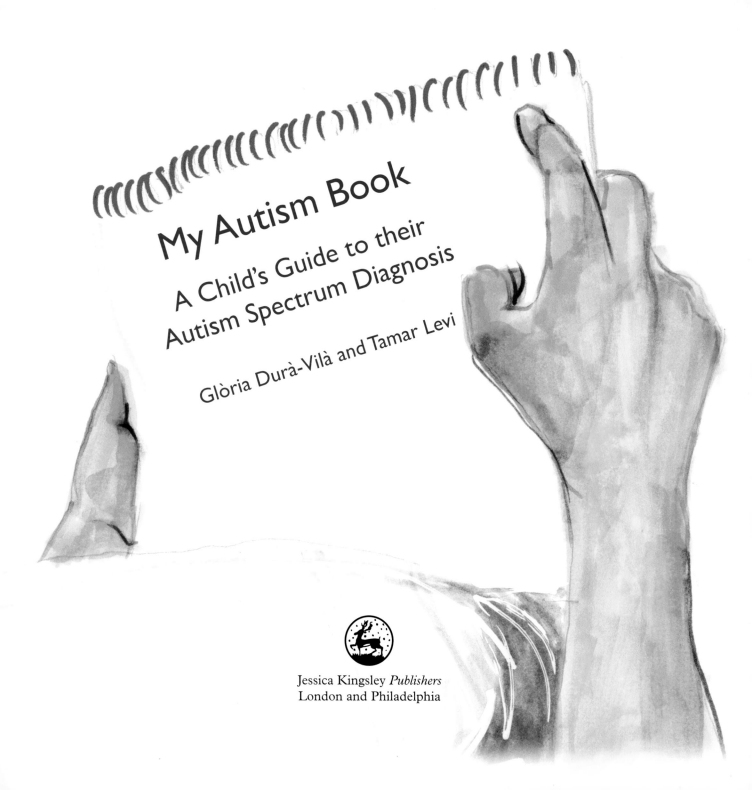

My Autism Book

A Child's Guide to their Autism Spectrum Diagnosis

Glòria Durà-Vilà and Tamar Levi

Jessica Kingsley *Publishers*
London and Philadelphia

First published in 2014
by Jessica Kingsley Publishers
73 Collier Street
London N1 9BE, UK
and
400 Market Street, Suite 400
Philadelphia, PA 19106, USA

www.jkp.com

Library of Congress Cataloging in Publication Data
A CIP catalog record for this book is available from the Library of Congress

British Library Cataloguing in Publication Data
A CIP catalogue record for this book is available from the British Library

ISBN 978 1 84905 438 6
eISBN 978 0 85700 868 8

Printed and bound in China

To David and our little darling boy Josep
from Glòria

To Sarah Levi, Dalia Levi and Vasilis Katsardis,
with gratitude and love
from Tamar

This is a letter to your parents. ➡

It could be called The Preface.

This means it's at the beginning of the book.

Ask your mum or dad to read this before you begin the book.

Letter to Parents

Dear Parents,

It's important to tell your child what having an Autism Spectrum Disorder (ASD) means and to get involved early with what ASD is for your child. This book aims to provide a starting point for communicating about ASD and answer the question 'What is my ASD?' Remember that every child on the autism spectrum is unique and has different abilities and difficulties.

This book has been written by a child psychiatrist and a children's author to help explain the diagnosis of ASD in a clear and positive way. The text is written in a matter-of-fact tone that children on the autism spectrum tend to appreciate most. The illustrations avoid facial expressions that they might find confusing. This book is for you to read together with your child if he or she has been diagnosed with ASD.

Find a space with few distractions. Choose a time when your child is in a receptive mood. It doesn't have to be read all at once and can be revisited any time.

Encourage your child to share this book with others such as close relatives, teachers and learning assistants. It can help your child and others understand his or her specific differences while nourishing and highlighting the strengths that he or she has noted here.

Enjoy!

Glòria Durà-Vilà and Tamar Levi

My Autism Spectrum Disorder

When you first find out that you have an Autism Spectrum Disorder it can be a bit confusing. This book will help you to find out what it means for you.

Having an Autism Spectrum Disorder is not like having an illness such as when you have a bad cold or chickenpox. It will not go away but it will not hurt you either. It means that you will find some things difficult and it also means that you will have some special strengths.

People who have these strengths and differences have what we call, using one big name, Autism Spectrum Disorder, or ASD for short. Having an Autism Spectrum Disorder is not your fault or your family's fault. It is not anyone's fault.

Each person's brain is different.

Hans Asperger

One of the first people who studied and wrote about the strengths and differences that you are experiencing was a man named Hans Asperger. You can see his picture on the next page.

Hans Asperger wrote a list of the strengths and differences that he noticed in the children he worked with. It was such a good list that one type of Autism Spectrum Disorder was named after him. It is called Asperger's Syndrome. Ask your doctor if your Autism Spectrum Disorder is the type called Asperger's Syndrome.

Whatever you call your Autism Spectrum Disorder, you can use this book to make your own list like Hans Asperger did! That's why it's called *My* Autism Book. In this book you can read some of the strengths and differences you may have noticed in yourself.

11

My Strengths and Differences

Having an Autism Spectrum Disorder will become easier as you learn what your difficulties are and how to make the most of your strengths. Every person with an Autism Spectrum Disorder has their own strengths and differences, so use this book to think about what it means for you.

Not everything written in this book may be true for you.

At the end of the book you can use a pencil to put a tick mark against the strengths and differences that you think are TRUE.

Here is an example of a strength that could be ticked:

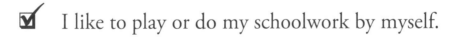 I like to play or do my schoolwork by myself.

13

Here is the beginning of the list:

You can be very honest.

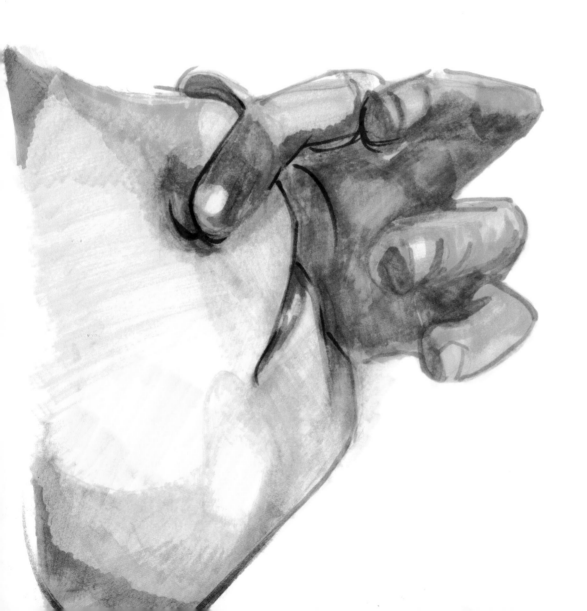

You don't like telling lies but sometimes telling
the truth gets you into trouble!

You may have strong powers of concentration.

Have you ever looked at something for longer than other people?

Sometimes you might find it difficult to understand feelings, facial expressions and turns of phrase.

You may also find it difficult to show your own feelings.

You may make good friends with adults or younger children.

Have you ever noticed that they can be better listeners
or are more willing to play the games that you want?

You might not like being in crowds. Or you might find you're not part of a group.

You may like to play or do your schoolwork by yourself.

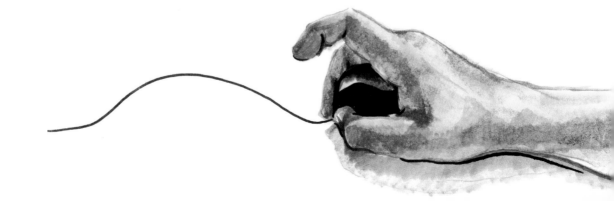

Your senses can seem stronger
than those of others.

22

You might not like making eye contact or shaking hands. You may not like kisses or being hugged either. Do you prefer to choose when you give hugs?

You might not like certain noises, fabrics or foods.

This may mean you have a favourite food.

Or a favourite piece of clothing that
you like better than any other.

You might not like change. For example, you might not like it when there is a change to your routine at home.

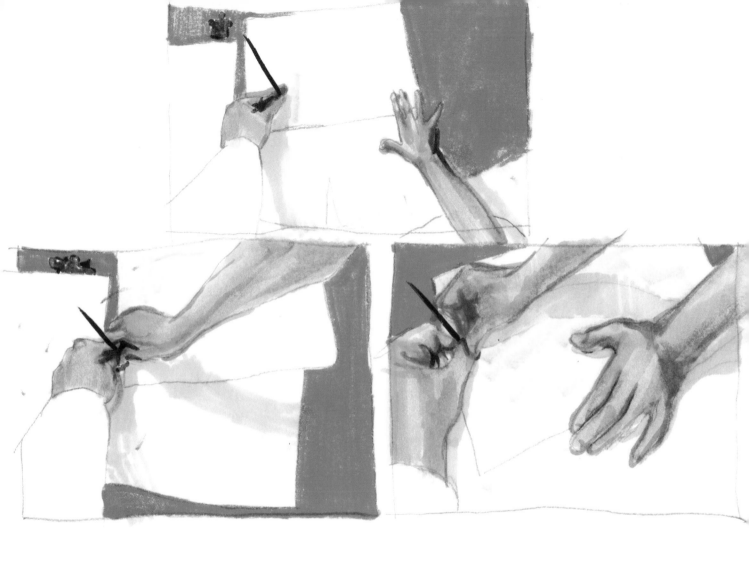

Or when there is a change to how you do things at school.

You may have special skills such as remembering dates.

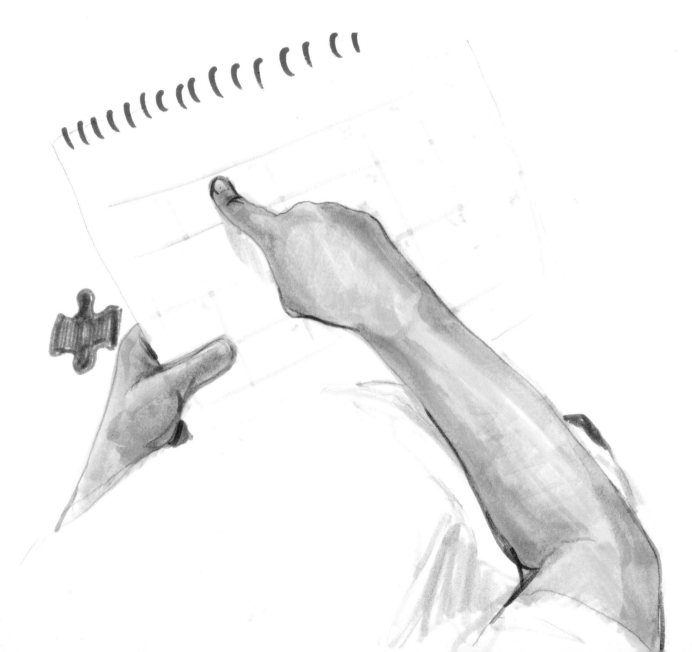

You might like lining things up or putting them in a certain order.

Some people give up quickly. You might
keep trying and trying and trying!

Some people get tired quickly. You might have a lot of energy!

Have you ever noticed that you are able to play for longer than other children?

You may get excited and speak too loudly or for too long.
Sometimes this might get you into trouble at school.

You may feel impatient when you have to wait
for your parents and teachers to help you.

You might have special interests.
Are there some things that you like doing more than anything else?

You might be very tidy with your favourite things.
Does it upset you when others do not take as
much care with your things as you do?

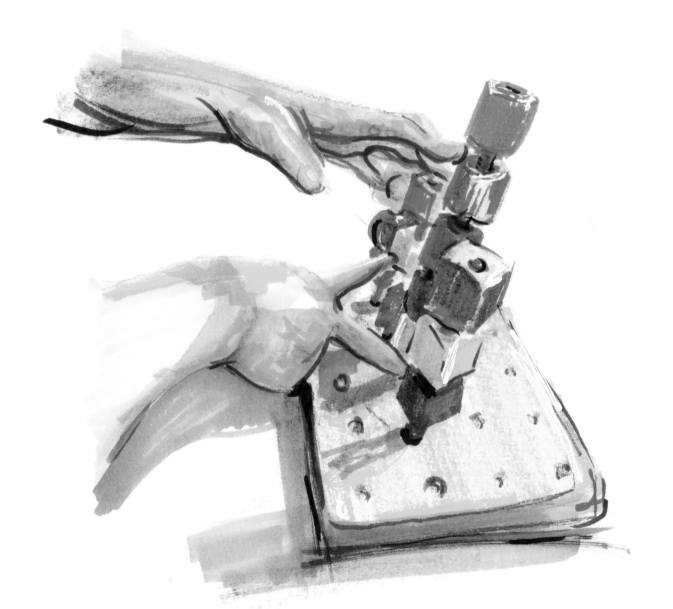

Sometimes you might not want to read storybooks. You may prefer to read books that are about facts, or things, or the past.

Do you prefer books about dinosaurs, trains, insects, animals, comics or games?

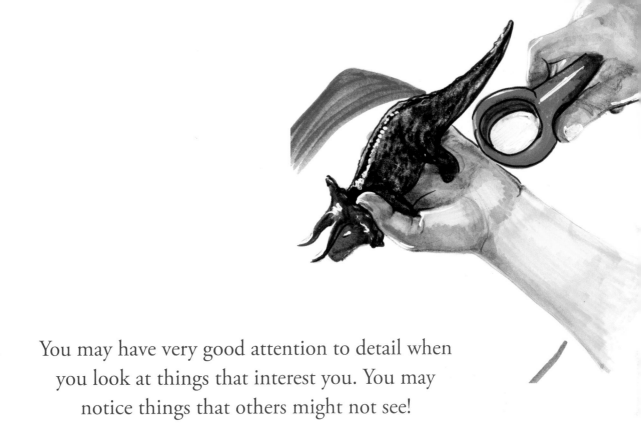

You may have very good attention to detail when you look at things that interest you. You may notice things that others might not see!

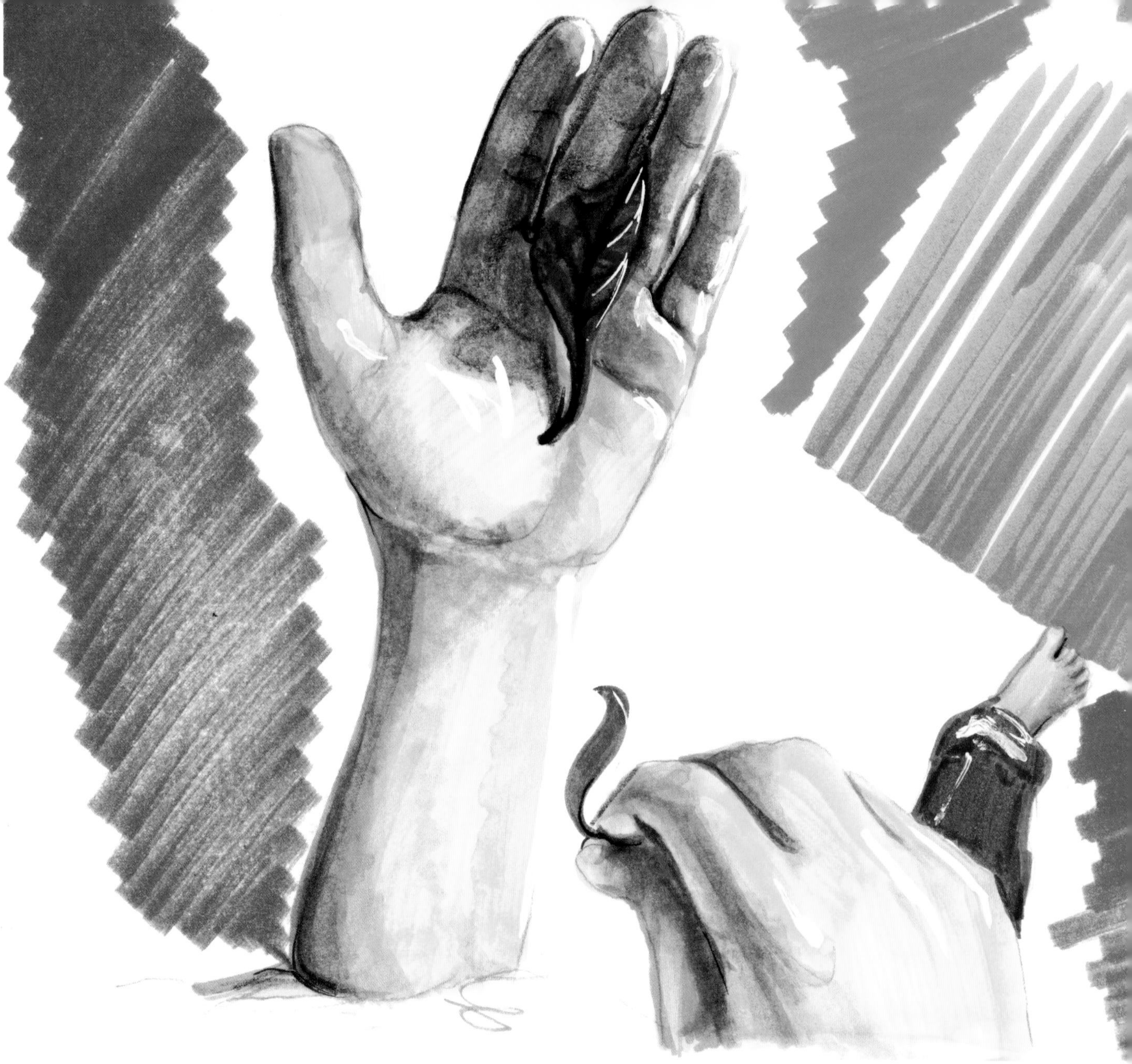

This is the end of the list.

Over the next four pages you will find a list of all of the strengths and differences that we have talked about in this book. Use a pencil to tick the strengths and differences that are true for you. Here is an example of a strength that could be ticked:

☑ I like to play or do my schoolwork by myself.

You can change these at any time. You can even add any that might not be in this book.

My Strengths and Differences

❑   I can be very honest.

❑   I have strong powers of concentration.

❑   I find it difficult to understand feelings, facial expressions and turns of phrase.

❑   I get along better with adults or younger children than with children my own age.

❑   I do not like being in crowds, and often feel that I am not part of a group.

❑   I like to play or do my schoolwork by myself.

❑ My senses seem stronger than those of others.

❑ I do not like making eye contact or being hugged.

I am sensitive to:

❑ loud noises

❑ itchy clothing

❑ lumpy food.

My favourite food is _____

My favourite item of clothing is _____

❑ I do not like it when there is a change to my routine at home or at school.

❑ I am really good at remembering dates.

❑ I like to line things up and put them in a certain order.

❑ I do not give up quickly. I keep trying and trying and trying!

❑ I have lots of energy.

❑ I sometimes get excited and speak too loudly or for too long.

❑ I feel impatient when I have to wait for help.

❑   I have special interests – things that I like
    doing more than anything else.

    My special interests are _____

    _____

❑   I am very tidy with my favourite things.

❑   I prefer to read books that are about
    facts, or things, or the past.

❑   I have very good attention to detail.

My Autism Spectrum Disorder
(at age_____)

My biggest strengths and differences are:

Strengths: _____

_____

_____

_____

Differences: _____

_____

_____

_____

If you'd like to, you can do a drawing of your differences, your strengths, or even yourself in the box below.

Here is another letter to your parents. ➡

It could be called The Epilogue.

This means it's at the end of the book.

Letter to Parents

Dear Parents,

As you can tell, there are a wide variety of strengths and differences. It may be useful to take a copy of the last few pages of this book and give it to special needs practitioners who might be working with your child.

You may also want to use it as a written plan of things to develop and things to celebrate with your child.

As you work towards this plan, and as your child grows, their strengths and differences may change. So, please encourage your child to re-read the list, erase the ticks they drew the first time around, write anything they'd like to add and share in revisiting this book as often as you like.

And don't worry. You are going to be amazing parents of this wonderful child with ASD.

All the very best,

Glòria Durà-Vilà and Tamar Levi